Memories of STEAM

THE FINAL YEARS

ROGER SIVITER
ARPS

First published in 2006 by
Sutton Publishing Limited · Phoenix Mill
Thrupp · Stroud · Gloucestershire · GL5 2BU

British Library Cataloguing in Publication Data
A catalogue record for this book is available from the British Library.

ISBN 0-7509-4411-0

All photographs from the author's collection unless otherwise indicated.

We start appropriately at the beginning of 1965 on 2 January of that year. Ex-SR class N 2–6–0
no. 31816 leaves Guildford with the 12.35 Redhill to Reading train. This was the penultimate day of
steam haulage on this route. This mixed-traffic locomotive class was designed by Maunsell for the
South Eastern & Chatham Railway (SEC) and was first in ... The class was withdrawn
from service in June 1966. (*Hugh Ballantyne*)

Title Page: Ex-LMS class 8F 2–8–0 no. 48710 climbs towards Copy Pit summit with a train of empty
coal wagons, 19 November 1966.

Typeset in 10/12 pt Palatino.
Typesetting and origination by
Sutton Publishing Limited.
Printed and bound in England by
J.H. Haynes & Co. Ltd, Sparkford.

Contents

By 1965 the ex-LNER Gresley A3 Pacific locomotives were not too common on the ground. However, one or two members of this famous class of locomotives (among which, of course, is *Flying Scotsman*) could still be found at work on the Waverley route, which ran between Carlisle, Hawick and Edinburgh. On 6 November 1965, within weeks of the end of regular steam working over the route, we see 4–6–2 no. 60052 *Prince Palatine* as it climbs up to Whitrope summit, just north of the lonely outpost of Riccarton Junction, with the 08.16 Edinburgh Millerhill to Carlisle freight train. Regular steam workings finished on this route at the end of 1965, and the line was closed in January 1969. (*Ken Hale*)

Introduction

The years 1965 to 1968 – steam on British Rail having finished by August 1968 – do not immediately conjure up visions of an abundance of steam workings. However, as can be seen in my previous volume *Farewell to Steam*, this was certainly not the case. For apart from certain areas, notably Devon and Cornwall, parts of Wales, Kent, East Anglia and the north of Scotland, there was still a great deal of steam working in the rest of the country, which over the final three and a half years would gradually disappear. And I stress *gradually* because, for example, steam on the Southern Region lasted until July 1967, parts of the north-east until September 1967, the Settle & Carlisle route and the West Coast Main Line over Shap until the very end of 1967, and right through until the summer months of 1968 there were still many areas of the north-west, notably around Manchester and Preston, where steam was still used on a regular daily basis. Add to this the many special trains that were run in this period, and you have a fine mix of steam activity.

Whereas in *Farewell to Steam* I divided the country up into areas, this time the reader will find that on each double-page spread the pictures are juxtaposed so that they relate to each other by theme.

In compiling this book I am once again very grateful to the photographers Ben Ashworth, Hugh Ballantyne, Peter Gray and Ken Hale for allowing me to use their pictures; to my wife Christina for much help; and last but not least to the BR staff who made it all possible.

Unless specified, all photographs were taken by me.

Roger Siviter, ARPS
Evesham, 2006

Opposite: Manchester Victoria station is the location as ex-LMS Stanier class 5MT 4–6–0 no. 44890 receives attention before leaving with an eastbound van train. The date is Saturday 9 March 1968.

Ex-GWR class 5100 2–6–2T no. 4147 speeds along the Birmingham Snow Hill to Kidderminster and Worcester line on 8 May 1965. The location is just south of Churchill & Blakedown station, and the train is the 17.05 Snow Hill to Hartlebury local service. From Monday 7 September 1964, all local trains out of Birmingham Snow Hill station were booked to be DMU. However, starting on 1 March 1965, a new steam working was introduced, the 07.59 Kidderminster to Snow Hill, with the return working being the 17.05 Snow Hill to Droitwich which ran on to Hartlebury on Saturdays only. This service lasted until the start of the winter timetable in September 1965. (See also photograph on page 49.) (*Ken Hale*)

Opposite: 'Jubilee' class 6P5F 4–6–0 no. 45593 *Kholapur* storms out of Leeds near Farnley & Wortley station with a Scarborough to Manchester summer Saturday train on 2 September 1967. These ex-LMS locomotives were designed by Sir William A. Stanier, FRS, and first introduced in 1934. They were withdrawn by the end of 1967 but several remain in preservation, including *Kholapur*, which is based at Tyseley. Note the 55A shed-plate – Leeds Holbeck. (*Ken Hale*)

Memories of Steam

These three views all show 'Britannia' Pacific locomotives at work on the West Coast Main Line (WCML).

The first (*above*) shows no. 70014 *Iron Duke* as it pulls away from Carlisle with the 08.00 Carlisle to Birmingham train. The date is 26 August 1967, and the exact location is where the WCML crosses over the Carlisle avoiding line from the east to the north and west of Carlisle Citadel station. (*Ken Hale*)

The second photograph (*opposite top*), taken on 28 May 1966, shows 4–6–2 no. 70051 *Firth of Forth* approaching Acton Grange Junction (just south of Warrington) with a down class C fitted goods train. (*Hugh Ballantyne*)

The final scene (*opposite below*) shows what has over the years become something of a famous train. The date is 26 December 1967 and, within a few days of the majority of the class being withdrawn, no. 70013 *Oliver Cromwell* (which survived withdrawal) heads away from Lancaster in beautiful winter sunshine with a Carlisle to Blackpool football special train. With the virtual withdrawal of the class and the end of steam over Shap by the end of December 1967, it is easy to see why this train has become a celebrity. (*Ken Hale*)

The former GWR Birmingham Snow Hill to Stourbridge Junction line still saw steam working throughout most of 1966, for although Stourbridge closed to steam on 11 July 1966, Tyseley shed remained open for steam until November of that year. One of the most interesting locations on this route was Old Hill bank, which ran for over a mile between Old Hill and Rowley Regis stations, with a ruling gradient of 1 in 70 also running through Old Hill tunnel, which is around half a mile long. These three photographs were taken on the bank about a quarter of a mile east of Old Hill station, on the morning of 6 April 1966.

Although, apart from the 0–6–0 pannier tanks, the GWR locomotives had now finished on the route, there were still plenty of ex-LMS class 8F 2–8–0 freight locomotives, both to haul the goods trains and to provide banking assistance up the 1 in 70 gradient. The first photograph (*above*) shows a heavy freight from Stourbridge Junction to Birmingham (hauled by 8F no. 48061) being banked by 8F no. 48121.

A few minutes later, and we see 8F 2–8–0 no. 48410, first of all as it approaches the camera (*opposite top*), and then as it approaches Old Hill tunnel, with a Birmingham-bound goods train (*opposite below*).

The Southern Region shed at Weymouth (71G) is our next location. This photograph taken on 21 August 1966 shows Bulleid 'West Country' class 4–6–2 no. 34034 *Honiton* with a brace of Standard class 4MT 2–6–4Ts, the one on the right being no. 80085. These Standard tank locomotives were designed at Brighton and first introduced in 1951. (*Ben Ashworth*)

On the early morning of 7 April 1966, Standard class 4MT 2–6–4T no. 80152 is seen inside Salisbury shed (72B). Behind the tank locomotive is Standard class 4MT 2–6–0 no. 76007. This shed always had a good reputation for the turnout of its locomotives, which is well illustrated here.

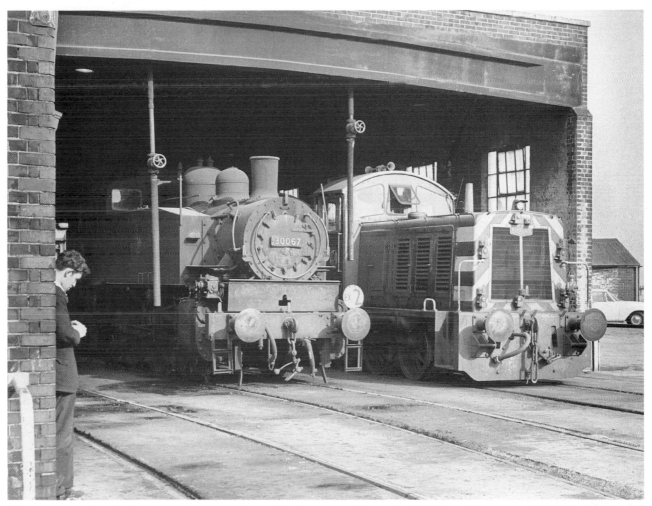

The final view in this Southern shed trio shows Southampton Docks shed (71I) on 21 August 1966. Next to the BR Ruston & Hornsby 0–6–0 diesel shunter is ex-SR class 3F USA 0–6–0T no. 30067. These locomotives were introduced in 1942 for the US Army Transportation Corps. They were then purchased by the SR in 1946, who modified the cabs and bunkers, as well as making other alterations. (*Ben Ashworth*)

The summer of 1966 was to be the 'swansong' of the famous Gresley A4 class Pacific locomotives, their last home being in Scotland to work the Glasgow to Aberdeen trains. These were mainly the three-hour trains, which required smart running between the two cities. The three remaining A4 Pacifics working the summer timetable of 1966 were nos 60019 *Bittern*, 60024 *Kingfisher* and 60034 *Lord Faringdon*. I should also add that A2 Pacific no. 60532 *Blue Peter* was often to be seen on 'The Grampian', the 13.30 train from Aberdeen, with arrival in Glasgow (after numerous stops) at 17.30.

At midday on 14 June 1966, no. 60034 (*above*) is seen being coaled at Aberdeen Ferryhill shed (61B). It had earlier arrived in Aberdeen with the 08.25 three-hour service from Glasgow, and was being prepared to take the 13.30 'Grampian' service back to Glasgow.

The following day (15 June) sees no. 60019 *Bittern* at Mildens crossing (*opposite top*), just east of Forfar, with the 17.15 Aberdeen to Glasgow three-hour train.

No. 60024 *Kingfisher* works hard shortly after leaving Stonehaven on 9 July 1966 with the 17.15 Aberdeen to Glasgow train (*opposite below*). (*Final picture: Ken Hale*)

Water stop at Carnforth. The driver of 'Britannia' Pacific no. 70011 *Hotspur* looks on as the fireman finishes the age-old ritual of taking water, while pausing at Carnforth station on 18 June 1966 with a down morning parcels train. The BR Standard 7P6F 'Britannia' class 4–6–2s were first introduced in 1951. No. 70011 was built at Crewe works in May 1951 and withdrawn from service in December 1967. It spent most of its working life in East Anglia, its first shed being at Norwich (32A), but finished its working days at Carlisle Kingmoor shed (12A). (*Ben Ashworth*)

Another platform end scene, this time at Preston station on the afternoon of Sunday 25 February 1968, as the crew of 'Black Five' 4–6–0 no. 45345 wait to leave with the 17.52 train to Liverpool Lime Street.

During the final years of BR steam, many steam special trains were run over a good many parts of the BR network, using not only the existing BR steam fleet but sometimes locomotives that had been preserved. One such occasion was on 17 September 1966, when there was a Great Western Society special from Birmingham to Taplow (for its Open Day) and return, hauled by newly preserved ex-GWR 'Manor' class 4–6–0 no. 7808 *Cookham Manor*. The train is seen here on the return journey as it climbs up Hatton bank. This locomotive was built in 1938 and withdrawn from service in December 1965, when it was purchased in running order by P.A. Lemar and put into the care of the Great Western Society at its Didcot depot.

Another preserved GWR locomotive, this time 'Castle' class 4–6–0 no. 4079 *Pendennis Castle*, heads north near Cosford on the GWR Wolverhampton to Shrewsbury line on Saturday 4 March 1967 with 'The Birkenhead Flier' from Paddington, organised by Ian Allan. This train was one of four specials run that weekend to mark the end of through workings between Paddington, Birmingham and Birkenhead.

Looking slightly the worse for wear but apparently steaming effortlessly, ex-GWR 'Castle' class 4–6–0 no. 7029 *Clun Castle* climbs up Hatton bank on 12 November 1966 with a special train from Waterloo to Stratford-upon-Avon (via Oxford), from where (*below*) 'Britannia' Pacific no. 70004 *William Shakespeare* took the train forward to Birmingham Snow Hill and then on to Stourbridge Junction for Stourbridge Town. No. 70004 is seen near Henley-in-Arden on this section of the journey. This train, organised by the Locomotive Club of Great Britain (LCGB), returned to London Victoria via High Wycombe. (*Lower picture: Ken Hale*)

This photograph was taken at Waterloo station on 5 June 1967, just a few weeks before the end of steam on the Southern Region, and shows BR Standard class 4MT 2–6–4 no. 80015 shunting empty coaching stock. Waterloo was the last of the London termini to see regular steam working.

Just over a year earlier at Waterloo station, and we see 'West Country' Pacific no. 34021 (formerly *Dartmoor*) in very poor external condition, but obviously still in good running order, having just arrived at the London terminal's platform 10 at 13.00 with a morning train from Bournemouth on the old Whit Sunday, 29 May 1966.

Ex-SR class 8P 'Merchant Navy' Pacific no. 35014 *Nederland Line* speeds through the New Forest near Brockenhurst with a Bournemouth to Waterloo express on 10 September 1966. This famous class of locomotive, designed by Bulleid, was introduced in 1941 with a streamlined air-smoothed casing. From 1956 they were all rebuilt with Walschaerts valve gear and modified details, and the air-smoothed casing was removed. (*Ken Hale*)

On 29 October 1966, ex-LNER class J27 0–6–0 no. 65894 lifts a heavy train of empty coal wagons up the 1 in 45 of Seaton bank on its journey from Sunderland to South Hetton. Steam working in the north-east lasted until September 1967. (*Ken Hale*)

These two views were taken at Scots Gap on 23 June 1966 on the North British line from Morpeth to Woodburn. In the first, class J27 0–6–0 no. 65814 approaches the fine-looking Scots Gap station with the Thursday-only 10.25 Morpeth to Woodburn goods train, run to service the TA camp at Woodburn. Note the NB signal-box and the NB lower quadrant signals, and also the station trolley.

The second scene shows the train taking water at Scots Gap on that very wet June day.

These lovely old North Eastern 0–6–0 locomotives were first introduced in 1906, and designed by William Worsdell.

On Saturday 19 November 1966, ex-LMS class 8F 2–8–0 no. 48710 storms out of Summit tunnel and climbs towards Copy Pit summit with a train of empty coal wagons from the Burnley area to Todmorden and the West Riding of Yorkshire. With Rose Grove shed (10F) at Burnley being one of the last sheds to close, steam consequently survived on this route until the very end.

Although Halesowen to Longbridge (on the LMS Birmingham to Bristol line) had closed in 1963, the section from Halesowen to Old Hill (on the GWR Birmingham to Kidderminster line) remained open until 1969, with steam being used until the closure of Tyseley shed in November 1966. As these three photographs show, some of the very last of the ex-GWR 0–6–0 pannier tanks would often work this branch line.

The first photograph (*opposite top*), taken on 14 October 1966, shows class 5700 0–6–0 pannier tank no. 9774 as it banks the afternoon goods to Stourbridge (hauled by no. 4616) up the heavy grade out of Halesowen.

In the second view (*opposite below*), taken on 26 September 1966, ex-GWR class 5700 0–6–0 pannier tank no. 4696 waits on the branch near the short Old Hill tunnel with the afternoon goods to Stourbridge.

The final scene (*above*), taken on 16 August 1966, shows yet another class 5700 pannier tank, no. 3607, once again banking the afternoon Stourbridge goods, which is hauled by no. 4646 of the same class.

Manchester Exchange station is the location as ex-LMS class 8F 2–8–0 no. 48652 runs through with a westbound freight on 10 June 1968. As can be seen, this platform connects Exchange station with Victoria station, and before the closure of Exchange in 1969 it was the longest platform in the UK. Although known as no. 11, it actually comprised Victoria's no. 11, no. 11 Middle (which joins the two stations) and Exchange's no. 3, with a total length of 2,194ft. (*Ben Ashworth*)

Also on 10 June 1968, one of the surviving 'Britannia' Pacifics, no. 70013 *Oliver Cromwell*, runs westbound through Victoria station. (*Ben Ashworth*)

Earlier in 1968, on 9 March, class 5MT 4–6–0 no. 44890 waits to leave platform 17 at Manchester Victoria station with an eastbound van train. Note the old station benches and also, in front of the locomotive, what looks like a very old portable ladder.

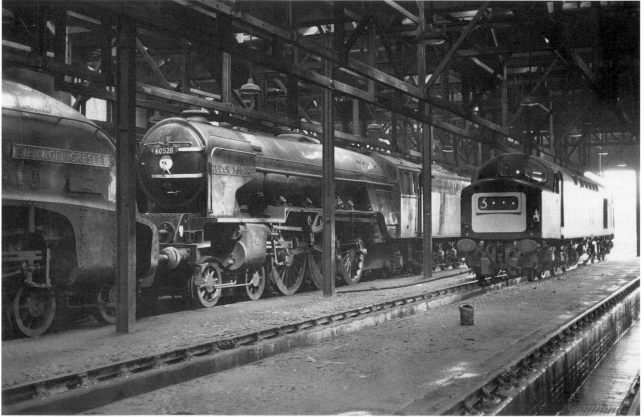

As with the Gresley A4 Pacific locomotives, the ex-LNER class A2 Pacifics also finished their days in Scotland in the summer of 1966. Three examples were to be seen: nos 60528 *Tudor Minstrel*, 60530 *Sayajirao* and 60532 *Blue Peter*.

The first photograph (*opposite top*) shows the front end of no. 60530 at Dundee shed (62B) on 17 June 1966. This locomotive worked very infrequently in the last months, and was mainly on standby duty at Dundee shed.

On 14 June 1966, no. 60528 (*opposite below*) rests in Ferryhill shed (61B), Aberdeen, alongside an English Electric class 40 diesel, and A4 Pacific no. 60007 *Sir Nigel Gresley*, which had recently been withdrawn from service and was destined for preservation.

The final scene (*above*) shows the only member of the A2 class to be preserved. No. 60532 *Blue Peter* is caught by the camera as it heads the 13.30 Aberdeen to Glasgow train near Plean junction, south of Stirling, on 18 June 1966. These extremely powerful locomotives (tractive effort 40,430lb) were introduced in 1947, and were an A.H. Peppercorn development of an earlier Thompson design.

Sadly, the Somerset & Dorset Joint Railway (S&DJR) between Bath and Bournemouth closed to traffic on 6 March 1966 but these four photographs, taken during 1965, show that this famous line was still going strong in its last full year.

The first view (*opposite top*) shows BR Standard class 4MT 2–6–4T no. 80138 leaving Bath Green Park station on 20 October 1965 with the 13.10 local train to Templecombe. The train is passing the Midland Railway shed; in the yard is BR Standard class 3MT 2–6–2T no. 82044, and behind the train are ex-LMS class 8F 2–8–0 no. 48525 and another class 3MT 2–6–2T, no. 82004. In the station platform can be seen 'Peak' class diesel locomotive no. D88 on a Bristol train.

On a beautiful spring afternoon, 10 April 1965, 2–6–4T no. 80039 (*opposite below*) crosses Tucking Mill viaduct (95 yards long and eight arches) with the 15.20 Bath to Templecombe local train. At the rear of the train is the down Midford distant signal.

The third view in this quartet of S&D pictures shows no. 80037 (*top*) leaving Evercreech Junction on 31 July 1965 with the 16.20 Templecombe to Bath train.

The last busy scene was taken at Evercreech Junction (*above*) on 30 October 1965. No. 80041 with the 08.15 Bath to Templecombe is being replenished with water, while on the left-hand side class 4MT 2–6–0 no. 76026 waits to leave on the 09.00 Templecombe to Bath service. On the centre track class 2MT 2–6–2T no. 41283 waits to work the 09.55 branch train from Evercreech to Highbridge, the junction for the Highbridge branch being just north of Evercreech Junction. (*All four photographs: Hugh Ballantyne*)

By the beginning of 1966, with the wholesale withdrawal of the GWR 4–6–0 locomotives at the end of 1965, some steam-hauled passenger services on ex-GWR lines were hauled by LMS class 5MT 4–6–0s, including the Shrewsbury to Chester section of the Paddington to Birkenhead line. This would be the case until the end of the through services from Paddington on 5 March 1967. On 7 May 1966, 'Black Five' 4–6–0 no. 45275 speeds across the impressive-looking Chirk viaduct, just north of Gobowen, with a Chester to Shrewsbury passenger train. This sixteen-arch viaduct crosses over the River Ceiriog and also the border into England. At the eastern side of the viaduct and almost touching it but a little lower is Telford's canal aqueduct, which carries the Shropshire Union Canal. (*Ken Hale*)

Ex-LMS class 5MT 4–6–0 no. 45013 makes a splendid sight as it climbs out of Penrith on the WCML with the 07.10 Carlisle to Banbury freight on 4 November 1967. As with the previous photograph, fine use of the telephoto lens is demonstrated here. In the mid-1960s, it was still quite rare to see these types of lenses being used in railway photography and Ken Hale, along with a few other young photographers including notably his friend the late Paul Riley, was among the earliest to do so. (*Ken Hale*)

On 4 August 1966, ex-LMS class 8F 2–8–0 no. 48662 bursts out of Millfield tunnel, just north of Duffield on the Derby to Chesterfield line, with an afternoon northbound goods train. These powerful locomotives, which were the backbone of the LMS freight service, were designed by Stanier and introduced in 1935. With their 4ft 8½in driving wheels and tractive effort of 32,440lb, they were sometimes used on passenger workings. They lasted right until the very end of steam on BR, and several examples have been preserved.

Just south of Friden on the Cromford & High Peak Railway (C&HPR), where the line crossed the A5012 Cromford to Newhaven road on a level-crossing. Class J94 0–6–0ST no. 68006 hauls a train of empties from Friden to Middleton quarry on Friday 20 May 1966. The C&HPR railway closed on Sunday 30 April 1967 with no. 68006, together with no. 68012 of the same class, hauling a series of special trains on the line to mark the event. (See also the photograph on page 137.)

At the northern end of the C&HPR was Parsley Hay station and exchange sidings, which was also the junction station for the former LNWR Buxton to Ashbourne line. Class 2MT 2–6–0 no. 46480 pulls away from Parsley Hay on 20 May 1966 with a freight from Middleton quarry to Buxton. The line to Ashbourne had closed in 1963.

Steam workings on the Southern Region to Exeter and beyond had more or less finished by the early part of 1965, and so until the end of Southern steam in July 1967 the seaside resort and port of Weymouth became steam's last outpost in the south-west of England. On 21 August 1965, BR Standard class 5MT no. 73115 *King Pellinore* climbs Upway bank out of Weymouth and approaches Bincombe tunnel with the up Channel Islands boat express. It was common practice for trains to be banked up this steep gradient, which had grades of between 1 in 50 and 1 in 74, and on this occasion assistance was provided by ex-SR rebuilt 'Battle of Britain' class Pacific no. 34071 *601 Squadron*. (*Hugh Ballantyne*)

Ex-SR 'West Country' Pacific no. 34024 (formerly *Tamar Valley*) approaches Hamworthy Junction, just to the west of Bournemouth, with the lightweight 11.25 Weymouth to Waterloo service on 19 February 1966. (*Hugh Ballantyne*)

On 20 March 1966, the Railway Correspondence & Travel Society (RCTS) ran a special train in the Solent area. It started at Waterloo and ran to Salisbury, Southampton Docks, Fawley, Southampton Central, Fareham, Gosport, Havant and back to Waterloo.

The first photograph (*above*) shows the train arriving at Fareham behind BR Standard class 4MT 4–6–0 no. 75070. This locomotive then came off and, as shown in the second view (*below*), the train went down the Gosport branch behind ex-SR U class 2–6–0 no. 31639. This locomotive then hauled the special back to Fareham, and then double-headed with no. 75070 for the journey to Waterloo.

The U class 2–6–0s were designed by Maunsell and introduced in 1928. They were withdrawn in June 1966. (*Both photographs: Hugh Ballantyne*)

'West Country' Pacific no. 34040 *Crewkerne*
looks in fine fettle as it speeds along
near Winchfield with an up express on
15 October 1966.

These locomotives, designed by Bulleid,
were first introduced in 1945, and were
fitted with air-smoothed casing. In 1957,
several examples were rebuilt with
Walschaerts valve gear, modified details
and the air-smoothed casings removed.
(*Ken Hale*)

Steam remained on the former GWR Cambrian lines in mid-Wales until the end of the through working from Paddington on 4/5 March 1967. BR Standard class 4MT 4–6–0s nos 75022 and 75010 brighten up a dull day as they head through a steep cutting on the 1 in 52 of Talerddig bank. The train is the up 'Cambrian Coast Express' from Aberystwyth/Pwllheli to Paddington, and the date is Saturday 27 August 1966.

The up 'Cambrian Coast Express' again, this time on Saturday 6 August 1966, hauled by no. 75013. The location is Trewern, just east of Welshpool on the border between Montgomeryshire and Shropshire. In the background is Breidden Hill.

Saturday 20 August 1966 was a beautiful day and arguably there was nowhere better to be than on Talerddig bank, between Machynlleth and Caersws, with steam still holding sway on this ex-Cambrian/GWR line in picturesque mid-Wales. Class 4MT 4–6–0s nos 75055 and 75060 with the 10.30 Pwllheli to Birmingham have less than a mile to go before reaching the summit of Talerddig bank; the exact location is milepost 62. It looks as if no. 75055 has been specially cleaned, probably by the 'Neverers', led by Ken Hale. This group of young men, known as the 'Master Neverers' Association' (MNA), would spend hours cleaning locomotives in order to obtain the 'master shot'.

Although regular steam working had finished on the Waverley route at the end of 1965, several steam special trains were run, especially throughout 1966. One such special train was run by the Scottish Region on 3 December 1966, and featured ex-LNER class B1 4–6–0 no. 61278, seen here running north near Riccarton Junction. (*Ken Hale*)

On 30 October 1965, ex-LNER class V2 2–6–2 no. 60955 labours up to Whitrope summit, north of Riccarton Junction, with the 14.12 Carlisle Kingmoor to Edinburgh Millerhill freight. These powerful locomotives were designed by Gresley and introduced in 1936. During the war years (1939–45) they were well known for being used on very heavy passenger trains on the East Coast Main Line (ECML), taking as many as twenty coaches out of Kings Cross. (*Ken Hale*)

With Arnton Fell in the background, class 5MT 4–6–0 no. 45061 climbs up to Riccarton Junction with the 14.12 Carlisle Kingmoor to Edinburgh Millerhill goods train on 6 November 1965. (*Ken Hale*)

Although regular steam workings over the Waverley route had finished by the end of 1965, steam was still to be found at the southern end of the route, namely on the Langholm branch. This branch ran for 7 miles north from Riddings Junction, which was 14 miles from Carlisle on the Waverley line. Steam finished when the branch, which had been opened in 1864 (two years after the opening of the Waverley route), closed on 18 September 1967. These three photographs show the Carlisle Kingmoor to Langholm goods at work on Friday 21 July 1967, just weeks before closure of the branch.

The first scene (*opposite top*) shows ex-LMS Ivatt class 4MT 2–6–0 no. 43106 with the outward working from Carlisle, on the main line just south of Riddings Junction.

Next is no. 43106 in Langholm station (*opposite below*), waiting to return to Carlisle with the goods train which ran on Mondays, Wednesdays and Fridays only.

The final scene (*above*) shows no. 43106 climbing out of Langholm at the start of its journey back to Carlisle Kingmoor.

At the time that these photographs were taken, no. 43106 was shedded at Carlisle Kingmoor (12A) but soon after was transferred to Lostock Hall shed, Preston (10D). It was withdrawn on 23 June 1968 and then bought by eighteen members of the Severn Valley Railway, and made its debut at the SVR Open Days on 1–2 September 1968. (*All three photographs: Ken Hale*)

On 11 March 1965, ex-GWR 'Hall' class 4–6–0 no. 6956 (formerly *Mottram Hall*) crosses the River Wye at Chepstow with a down freight. By the end of 1965, this class of locomotive would all have been withdrawn from service, with no. 6956, which was built in 1943, one of the last to go, being withdrawn in December. Happily, several members of the class survive in preservation and are often seen on main-line charter trains. (*Ben Ashworth*)

Ex-GWR class 4MT 2–6–2T no. 4178 approaches Old Hill station on 20 August 1965 with the 07.59 Kidderminster to Birmingham Snow Hill commuter train. (See also photograph on page 6.) These sturdy-looking tank locomotives, introduced in 1929, were a modified design by Collett from the Churchward 3100 class (introduced in 1903) and were used mainly on suburban passenger workings, especially round the Birmingham and Midlands area. (*Ken Hale*)

The location is the atomic flask loading point near Berkeley power station, Gloucestershire. On 31 August 1965, ex-GWR 'Manor' class 4–6–0 no. 7829 (formerly *Ramsbury Manor*) pauses during shunting duties. No. 7829 was the last member of the class, which was designed by Collett and first introduced in 1938. No. 7829 was, however, built in December 1950 and withdrawn in December 1965. Several examples were preserved, but not no. 7829. (*Ben Ashworth*)

Gresley LNER class A3 Pacific no. 4472 *Flying Scotsman*, probably the most famous steam locomotive in the world, looks a treat and receives admiring glances while it pauses in York station after bringing in the 'White Rose' special charter train from King's Cross on Sunday 1 May 1966. This fine-looking locomotive, the only member of this class (first introduced in 1927) to be preserved, is still going strong today. Note also the elegance of this splendid station and its beautiful overall roof.

BR Standard class 7P6F 'Britannia' no. 70013 *Oliver Cromwell* pauses at Manchester Victoria station on Saturday 1 June 1968, after bringing in the BR Scottish Region 'Grand Rail Tour No. 5' from Edinburgh, the 'Britannia' Pacific having come onto the train at Carnforth. No. 70013 then worked the special train to Hellifield, where diesel traction took over for the return journey.

We complete this trio of large station photographs at the ex-GWR Birmingham Snow Hill station, which closed in 1972 (the new station opened on the same site in 1987). On 30 April 1966, class 5MT 4–6–0 no. 44872 enters the lovely old station with the annual Ffestiniog Railway special train from Paddington to Portmadoc. I spent many happy hours train-spotting at this spacious station in the late 1940s and will always remember it with great affection.

On the afternoon of 30 April 1966, BR Standard class 4MT 2–6–0 no. 76036 approaches Water Orton (to the east of Birmingham) from the Derby area with a westbound coal train. The lines on the right-hand side run to Nuneaton and Leicester. Note the 'spotters' on the lengthy wall, behind which are one or two of what we now call 'old' cars, including a Morris Minor Traveller and what looks like a Ford Prefect. In the background are the many cooling towers of Hams Hall power station, which was demolished in about 1990 and is now a freight terminal.

Opposite: BR steam working in south-west Scotland (mostly around the Ayrshire coalfields) continued until the close of Ayr shed (67C) at the end of 1966.

On 24 June 1966, BR class 4MT 2–6–0 no. 76100 (*top*) is seen climbing out of Ayr near Annbank Junction with empty coal wagons for Mauchline.

The second photograph (*below*), also taken on 24 June 1966, shows another BR Standard class 4MT 2–6–0, this time no. 76074, as it drifts down the bank and approaches Annbank Junction with a train of empty coal wagons from the Mauchline direction. The BR class 4MT 2–6–0 locomotives were designed at Swindon, and first introduced in 1952. The last example of the class was withdrawn in December 1967. However, three members of the class have been preserved.

These two photographs were taken on 1 June 1968 at Manchester Victoria station. The first (*opposite*) shows 'Black Five' 4–6–0 no. 45206 shunting parcels vans in one of Victoria's bay platforms.

The second scene (*above*) shows another member of this famous 4–6–0 class, no. 45156, as it reverses out of Victoria station after bringing in an empty stock train and heads west for its home base at Patricroft shed (9H). This shed and Newton Heath (9D) were the last steam sheds in Manchester, and both of them closed at the end of June 1968. No. 45156 was named *Ayrshire Yeomanry*, one of only four members of the class to receive names.

The Stanier 'Black Five' 4–6–0s were first introduced on the LMS in 1934, and were built over several years until the final total reached 841, the highest number in any locomotive class on BR. They worked right until the end of BR steam, no. 45110 working the last section between Manchester and Liverpool of the 11 August 1968 BR 'Fifteen Guinea Special'. Several examples of the class have been preserved, including no. 45110.

Ex-LNER class J27 0–6–0 no. 65809 trundles across the River Wansbeck viaduct, south of the Northumberland former mining town of Ashington, with a coal train bound for Cambois power station on 1 June 1966. This power station is situated near North Blyth on the mouth of the River Blyth. This photograph also shows well the American-style cab on these former North Eastern Railway 0–6–0s. They were withdrawn from service by the end of 1967. However, one example is preserved, no. 2392 (formerly no. 65894, which appears on page 22). (*Hugh Ballantyne*)

Another pre-grouping class of locomotive at work in the latter years of BR steam was the class O2 0–4–4T, which worked on the Isle of Wight on the remaining line from Ryde Pier Head to Shanklin, the other lines, with the exception of the privately preserved line between Wootton and Havenstreet, having closed by the end of 1965. No. 33 *Bembridge* enters Brading station with the 13.19 Ryde to Shanklin train on 21 July 1966. These vintage tank locomotives were introduced on the London & South Western Railway (LSWR) in 1889 and were designed by Adams.

On 31 December 1966, the last day of steam working on the Isle of Wight, class O2 0–4–4Ts no. 24 *Calbourne* and no. 31 *Chale* stand at Shanklin station before returning to Ryde Pier Head with an LCGB 'Farewell Special' train. The steam locomotives were replaced by London Tube trains. (*Hugh Ballantyne*)

While on the Isle of Wight on Thursday 21 July 1966, I came across this elderly looking railway crane, which was parked on a short siding near Brading station.

Ex-GWR class 5700 0–6–0PT no. 9610 stops for water on the single-track section between Brymbo steelworks and Minera limestone works, with the Tuesdays, Thursdays and Saturdays only 08.20 Wrexham Croes Newydd to Minera goods train on Saturday 7 May 1966. This steam working ran until the late spring of 1967, when Croes Newydd shed (6C) was closed to steam on 5 June. The class 5700 pannier tanks were introduced in 1929, and designed by Collett. (*Ken Hale*)

Another ex-GWR 0–6–0PT, this time a member of the 1600 class. No. 1638 is seen near Trevor on 31 May 1966 with a return trip freight working from Llangollen to Wrexham. This class of pannier tank was introduced in 1949 (just after nationalisation), and was designed by Hawksworth specially for light branch-line and shunting work.

Although the line from Wrexham to Llangollen has long been closed, the section westwards from Llangollen to Carrog (some 8 miles) has been preserved, and is known as the Llangollen Railway. (*Ken Hale*)

Ex-LMS Hughes/Fowler class 5MT 2–6–0 no. 42942 nears Denbigh with a special train from Rhyl to Denbigh on 24 September 1966. This train, which was organised by the LCGB, ran from Euston to Llandudno Junction, Blaenau Ffestiniog, Llandudno, Rhyl, Denbigh, Rhyl, Crewe and back to Euston, and was known as the 'Conway Valley' tour. (See also top photograph on page 106.) The former LNWR line from Rhyl to Denbigh connected with the ex-GWR Wrexham to Bala Junction line at Corwen, to the west of Llangollen. Apart from the preserved line from Llangollen to Carrog, there is no trace of these two lines today. (*Ken Hale*)

The LNER class B1 4–6–0s were introduced in 1942, and designed by Edward Thompson. No. 61261 of that once-numerous class speeds along between Inverkeithing and Burntisland on the Edinburgh to Dundee line on 28 July 1966 with a down lightweight freight train. These and the following photographs overleaf well illustrate the variety of main line steam freight workings still to be seen and photographed during this latter period of BR steam. (*Photograph above: Ken Hale*)

Opposite top: Class J38 0–6–0 no. 65914 heads for Thornton Junction with a train of scrap metal and coal from the Dunfermline area. The location is Cluny, some 4 miles south-west of Thornton. The LNER class J38 0–6–0s were designed by Sir Nigel Gresley and introduced in 1926. No examples of the class survived into preservation, and all members of the class were withdrawn by April 1967.

Opposite below: On 24 June 1966, class 5MT 4–6–0 no. 45126, having paused to take on a banking locomotive in the shape of BR Standard class 4MT 2–6–0 no. 76098, pulls away from Beattock station with a Carlisle to Glasgow mixed freight working. Steam on the WCML between Carlisle and Glasgow lasted until the end of Scottish steam in May 1967. As can be seen, Beattock station was a fairly busy area, with on the left-hand side breakdown cranes, on the right-hand side a two-road locomotive shed (68D), built of stone with open doors, and to the right of that a small goods yard.

I mentioned on the previous page the variety of freight workings. These three photographs show steam at work on mineral and ore trains.

The first (*opposite*), taken on 13 August 1966, shows 'Black Five' 4–6–0 no. 45051 on Aynho water troughs, south of Banbury, with a train of ore from the Northamptonshire quarries to Birmingham and the 'Black Country'.

The next scene (*right*) shows class 8F 2–8–0 no. 48167 climbing the steep gradient near Long Barn with a heavy mineral train from Preston to Blackburn on 6 June 1968.

In the final photograph (*below*), BR Standard class 9F 2–10–0 no. 92093 nears Ais Gill summit on the Settle to Carlisle line with a heavy southbound mineral train from Long Meg sidings, which are situated north of Culgaith. The photograph was taken at 10.50 a.m. on 13 September 1966.

The class 9F 2–10–0s were designed at Brighton and introduced in 1954. No. 92093 was built at Swindon in 1957 and withdrawn from service in September 1967. No. 92220 of the class had the distinction of being the last steam locomotive built for BR. It was built at Swindon in March 1960, and named *Evening Star*. Several members of the class, including no. 92220, have been preserved.

The up 'Cambrian Coast Express' leaves Welshpool on Thursday 2 March 1967 with BR Standard class 4MT 4–6–0 no. 75048 in charge. The following Saturday, 4 March 1967, would see the end of steam on this route for over twenty years, steam returning on the Shrewsbury to Machynlleth and Barmouth/Aberystwyth lines in the summer of 1987. (*Ken Hale*)

4–6–0 no. 75029 hurries along near Trewern (to the east of Welshpool) with the up 'Cambrian Coast Express' on Saturday 25 October 1966. In the background is Breidden Hill.

These BR class 4MT 4–6–0s were designed at Brighton and introduced in 1951. They survived until the end of steam on BR in August 1968, and several examples have been preserved, including No. 75029, which was preserved by the eminent wildlife and railway artist David Shepherd. It was subsequently named *The Green Knight*.

By early 1968, BR steam workings were more or less confined to the north-west of England, and in consequence the locomotive sheds in that area would be among the last to house the – by then – dwindling band of steam locomotives still on BR's books.

One such shed that lasted until the very end of steam was Lostock Hall (10D) at Preston. At that depot (*opposite*) on Sunday 25 February 1968, 'Black Five' 4–6–0 no. 45345 receives last-minute attention before running up to Preston station to take out the 17.52 train to Liverpool, which by that time was one of the few regular steam-hauled passenger workings in the BR timetable.

The former Lancashire & Yorkshire Railway (L&YR) shed at Bolton (9K) closed at the end of June 1968, and a visit to that location (*above*) on 6 June 1968 showed a mix of ex-LMS 'Black Five' 4–6–0s and class 8F 2–8–0s, with also a Type 2 diesel interloper, the shed never having had an allocation of main-line diesels. On shed that day were 8Fs nos 48337 and 48773, and class 5MTs nos 44947, 45073, 45290 and 45318. The splendid factory chimney is worthy of note, as are the two cars, which look like a Morris Minor and a Reliant Regal, two famous names from the British motor industry of almost half a century ago.

Although regular steam workings on the Settle & Carlisle route had ceased by the beginning of 1968, with the closure of Carlisle Kingmoor shed (12A) on 1 January 1968, some ballast trains still ran to and from Swinden quarry on the old Grassington branch (which ran from Skipton) to Appleby.

The last steam-hauled freight from Swinden to Appleby occurred on 31 May 1968, as shown in these three photographs. The first scene (*above*) shows BR Standard class 4MT 4–6–0 no. 75019 (suitably cleaned for the occasion) leaving Swinden for Skipton, the second view (*opposite top*) shows the train approaching Skipton, and the final photograph (*opposite below*) shows no. 75019 as it climbs the 1 in 100 gradient out of Horton in Ribblesdale and heads for Appleby. (*All three photographs: Ken Hale*)

This atmospheric 'shed scene' was taken at Bristol Barrow Road shed (82E) on 28 March 1965, just a few months before the shed was closed. Clustered around the turntable are an unidentified ex-GWR class 38XX 2–8–0, ex-GWR 'Hall' class 4–6–0 no. 6937 (formerly *Conyngham Hall*), an unidentified ex-GWR class 5700 0–6–0 pannier tank, ex-LMS class 4F 0–6–0s nos 44264 and 44135, and finally an unidentified ex-GWR 'Modified Hall' class 4–6–0. Barrow Road was formerly a Midland Railway shed, and was taken over by the Western Region from the London Midland Region in 1958. It was then recoded from 22A to 82E. (*Peter Gray*)

On a very wintry 2 April 1966, 'Black Five' 4–6–0 no. 45227 waits to leave Leeds City station with the 13.18 train to Newcastle. Approaching the station is a 'Peak' class diesel with a northbound passenger train.

On the same day as the previous picture (2 April 1966), ex-LNER class Q6 0–8–0 no. 63344 is caught by the camera near Leeds Holbeck shed (55A) as it heads for that depot, having earlier arrived at Leeds City station with a local goods train.

These 0–8–0 locomotives were introduced on the North Eastern Railway in 1913 and designed by Sir Vincent Raven, who was its chief engineer from 1910 to 1922.

This snowy scene shows ex-LNER class A4 Pacific no. 60019 *Bittern* as it leaves Gleneagles station in blizzard conditions on 19 February 1966. The train is the 13.30 Aberdeen to Glasgow service. (*Ken Hale*)

Ex-LMS class 5MT 4–6–0 no. 44942 acts as station pilot at Banbury station on a very wet Saturday 16 April 1966. This modern-looking concrete and brick station was built in about 1958, and replaced the earlier station, which was mostly constructed of wood and, until its removal in 1952, had an overall roof.

A visit to Banbury shed on 26 February 1966 shows BR Standard class 9F 2–10–0 no. 92029 in the shed yard. Banbury was originally a GWR/Western Region shed, and numbered 84C. It was transferred to London Midland Region control in September 1963, and renumbered 2D. It closed to steam on 30 October 1966, and continued as a diesel stabling point for a short while afterwards.

Oxford shed (81F) closed in January 1966, and a visit there on Saturday 26 February 1966 showed a variety of withdrawn steam locomotives in the shed yard, including BR Standard class 5MT no. 73166 (*right*) and ex-GWR 'Hall' class 4–6–0 no. 6947 (formerly *Helmingham Hall*) and also the front end of modified 'Hall' class 4–6–0 no. 7909 (formerly *Heveningham Hall; below*). (*Both photographs: Ken Blocksidge/Roger Siviter collection*)

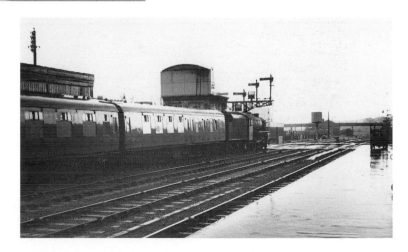

Throughout most of 1966, the York to Bournemouth trains were steam-hauled from Banbury to Bournemouth and return. On the same day as the previous two views, only now in very rainy conditions, 'Black Five' 4–6–0 no. 44860 prepares to leave Oxford station with the York to Bournemouth train, complete with Southern Region rolling stock.

A visit to Willesden locomotive shed (1A) on a very sunny 17 January 1965 shows quite a variety of locomotives. The photograph above gives some idea of the number of steam locomotives still allocated to this London shed, including, left to right, class 8F 2–8–0s nos 48624 and 48387, 'Black Five' 4–6–0s nos 45001 and 44771, and the bunker of class 3F 0–6–0T no. 47435 with no. 47432 behind it. The second scene, below, shows the front end of BR Standard class 2MT 2–6–0 no. 78019, 'Black Five' 4–6–0 no. 44833 and BR Standard class 4MT 2–6–0 no. 76041. Willesden shed closed in September 1965. (*Both photographs: Hugh Ballantyne*)

There was always something special about a visit to a steam locomotive shed on a Sunday, preferably late afternoon on a sunny day in the spring or summer months. This was just the case when I visited Crewe South shed (5B) on Sunday 24 April 1966. There was quite a variety of locomotives to be seen, including BR Standard class 2MT 2–6–0 no. 78036 and ex-LMS class 5MT 4–6–0 no. 45446. Other locomotives on shed that evening were 'Crab' 2–6–0 no. 42727, class 2MT 2–6–0 no. 78019, 'Britannia' class 4–6–2s nos 70012 and 70048, class 4MT 2–6–0 no. 76040, class 9F 2–10–0s nos 92002 and 92032, class 3F 0–6–0T no. 47521 and class 5MT 4–6–0 no. 45447, as well as several other locomotives which were inaccessible to me.

One of the last sheds to close was Rose Grove (10F), Burnley. On 19 July 1968, class 5MT 4–6–0 no. 45212 was photographed near the shed with a short breakdown train.

In the final years of BR steam, several locomotives were preserved; some would be used on the main line, a few would be in museums and several, especially the smaller locomotives, would find homes on the newly preserved branch lines which were springing up all over the UK. On Sunday 20 August 1967, recently preserved LNER class A4 Pacific no. 4498 *Sir Nigel Gresley* prepares to leave its home town of Doncaster with a special charter train for Edinburgh and return, organised by the owners of the locomotive, the A4 Locomotive Society. (See also lower photograph on page 30.)

The last few examples of the famous GWR 'Castle' class 4–6–0s were actually built in the early days of BR, including preserved no. 7029 *Clun Castle*. This was built in May 1950 and was one of the last members of the class to be withdrawn in December 1965, when it was straight away preserved by the Standard Gauge Steam Trust at Tyseley. Throughout most of 1966 it would often be found at work on trip freight workings between Birmingham and Banbury. It is seen here on 4 March 1967 climbing Gresford bank (just north of Wrexham) with a return special charter train from Chester to Paddington, run to mark the end of through workings between Paddington and Birkenhead. The 'Castle' class was introduced in 1923, and designed by C.B. Collett. (*Ken Hale*)

Opposite: Another preserved Pacific locomotive, this time ex-LMS 'Coronation' class 4–6–2 no. 46235 *City of Birmingham*, seen here near Saltley shed (Birmingham) on 19 May 1966, after arrival from Crewe works. Unlike no. 4498, no. 46235 was on its way to the Birmingham Science Museum for permanent display. In attendance is BR Type 2 diesel no. D5180. Behind the locomotive is Duddeston Road signal-box, and overlooking the scene is the fine Saltley gas works. The 'Coronation' class Pacifics were introduced in 1937, and designed by Stanier. Several members of the class were originally streamlined (including no. 46235), but the casings were removed in 1946.

Opposite and right: These two scenes were taken at St Johns (Ryde) on the Isle of Wight on 21 August 1966 and show, first of all, class 02 0–4–4T no. 27 *Merestone* waiting to leave the station with a Ryde to Shanklin train, and secondly no. 35 *Freshwater* in the shed yard. (*Both photographs: Ben Ashworth*)

Below: The third Isle of Wight photograph, taken earlier at St Johns on 21 July 1966, shows no. 14 *Fishbourne* and no. 17 *Seaview* inside the locomotive shed (70H), which also formed part of the works complex.

On a very wet 18 August 1967, 'Black Five' 4–6–0 no. 44917 approaches Preston station with an afternoon parcels train bound for Carlisle. Dominating this scene is the fine LMS gantry signal.

Another scene at Preston station, this time taken on 26 February 1968. Class 5MT 4–6–0 no. 44761 takes one of the through freight lines as it heads south with empty coal wagons. Partly obscured by smoke is another of Preston's gantry signals. With the electrification of the whole WCML, scenes like this, and the previous photograph, would soon become history.

Another fine gantry signal, this time of the Southern Railway variety. On a wet Maundy Thursday in 1966 (7 April), grimy ex-SR 'Battle of Britain' class 4–6–2 no. 34088 (formerly *213 Squadron*) pauses to take water at Basingstoke station with an afternoon up goods train to the London area. Note the junction in front of the train, the lines to the left going to Reading and the line straight ahead to Waterloo. Also note the ornate SR-style lamps of concrete construction.

Although the Seaton branch (ex SR) was dieselised in November 1963, owing to a shortage of DMUs steam returned on the branch for a short time in February 1965 (*above*), with two ex-GWR class 1400 0–4–2Ts, nos 1442 and 1450, plus autotrailer coaches.

On 27 February 1965, no. 1442 (*below*) is seen propelling its autotrailer into and out of Colyton station with a Seaton to Seaton Junction train. As can be seen, there had been sidings at this station, but they were removed in 1964.

The Class 1400 0–4–2Ts were introduced in 1932 and designed by Collett for light branch work and, as in these photographs, push-and-pull workings. No. 1442 is now in Tiverton Museum.

One further point: after closure of the branch in 1966, it was taken over by the Seaton Tramway (2ft 9in gauge), running first of all in 1970 from Seaton to Colyford, and then in 1979 to its northern terminus at Colyton. (*Both photographs: Peter Gray*)

The former SR branch line from Wareham (on the Bournemouth to Weymouth line) to the south coast resort of Swanage closed in 1972, but part of the line has been preserved and is known as the Swanage Railway. This almost aerial view, taken on 7 August 1965, shows class 2MT 2–6–2T no. 41316 approaching Corfe Castle with a Wareham to Swanage train. These locomotives were designed by H.G. Ivatt for the LMS and introduced in 1946. (*Peter Gray*)

Class 8F 2–8–0s nos 48191 and 48465 leave Chinley North Junction on
21 October 1967 with a mixed-goods train bound for Peak Forest, near
Buxton. These freight workings, mainly mineral trains, were worked
by steam until March 1968, when diesel traction took over. At the time,
this line was part of the through route from Manchester to Derby, but
this closed in 1968 leaving open Chinley to Peak Forest/Buxton at the
northern end (for freight only) and in the south Ambergate Junction to
Matlock. However, part of the line from Matlock to Rowsley was later
preserved, and is known as Peak Rail. (*Ken Hale*)

The last ex-GWR class 5600 0–6–2Ts nos 5605 and 6697 were withdrawn from Croes Newydd shed (6C), Wrexham, on 21 May 1966. A timely visit on Saturday 7 May 1966 shows no. 6697 still in nice external condition on the shed turntable. These powerful class 5MT locomotives were designed by Collett, mainly for service in the Welsh valleys, and were introduced in 1924. Several examples of the class have been preserved, including no. 6697 by the Great Western Society at Didcot. Behind no. 6697 is ex-GWR class 1600 (2F) 0–6–0PT no. 1628.

This view at Croes Newydd shed was taken on Monday 13 March 1967, and shows BR Standard class 4MT 4–6–0 no. 75002 receiving attention inside the shed. Croes Newydd shed closed on 5 June 1967.

These three photographs well illustrate the variety of ex-LNER locomotives still to be seen at work on the Scottish Region in the summer of 1966. The first (*opposite top*) shows A4 Pacific no. 60019 *Bittern* crossing Newtonhill viaduct, some 7 miles north of Stonehaven, with the 08.25 Glasgow to Aberdeen service on 30 May 1966. No. 60019 and no. 60034 were the last of this famous class to be withdrawn from service, in September 1966. The A4s were designed by Sir Nigel Gresley and introduced in 1935.

The second view (*opposite below*) was taken at Invergowrie on 29 July 1966, and shows V2 class 2–6–2 no. 60919 with the 08.29 Dundee to Perth empty coaching stock train as it crosses a bridge over a flooded quarry.

In the final photograph (*above*), class A2 Pacific no. 60532 *Blue Peter* is seen near Cumbernauld with the 13.30 Aberdeen to Glasgow train on 30 July 1966. This location is known as Cumbernauld Glen and is just north of Cumbernauld station, which is some 13¼ miles from Glasgow Buchanan Street station (which closed in November 1966). (*All three photographs: Ken Hale*)

On 13 July 1966, class 8F WD 2–8–0 no. 90135 approaches Wakefield from the Goole direction with a train of empty coal wagons. These powerful Ministry of Supply Austerity locomotives were designed by Riddles, and were introduced in 1943. They were purchased by British Railways in 1948 and were still active on BR until the end of 1967.

Opposite top: Another Wakefield scene, this time at the eastern end of Wakefield Kirkgate station. WD 2–8–0 no. 90649 enters the station on 22 September 1966 with a lengthy coal train from the Normanton area, bound for Healey Mills.

Opposite below: The WD 2–8–0s were still to be seen working around the Fife and Glasgow areas during 1966. On Saturday 18 June 1966, no. 90071 heads through Greenhill Junction station with an empty coal train from Glasgow to the Fife coalfields. Note the very high semaphore signal for sighting purposes.

The late-evening sunshine highlights 'Black Five' 4–6–0 no. 45394 as it climbs the 1 in 104 of Grayrigg bank with a heavy northbound freight on 16 September 1966. This bank runs from Oxenholme for 6 miles to the summit at Grayrigg, and on most occasions (but not this one) northbound freight workings had the assistance of banking locomotives, which were stationed at Oxenholme station (see next two photographs).

Opposite: The Fairburn class 4MT 2–6–4Ts were introduced in 1945 and were a development of an earlier Stanier design, with a shorter wheelbase and detail alteration. No. 42251 of the class banks a northbound goods up Grayrigg bank on Friday 17 September 1966. The train locomotive is 4–6–0 no. 45249. The banking locomotives were shedded at either Carnforth (10A) or Tebay (12E).

Oxenholme station on 18 June 1966, as class 5MT 4–6–0 no. 44987 pulls out of the busy station with a southbound passenger train. On the left is Fairburn class 4MT 2–6–4T no. 42210 awaiting the next banking duty up to Grayrigg summit. (*Ben Ashworth*)

Class 8F 2–8–0 no. 48775, BR Standard class 5MT 4–6–0 no. 73133, 'Black Five' 4–6–0 no. 45187 and an unidentified 8F 2–8–0 pose in Patricroft shed (9H) on 1 June 1968. This shed together with Newton Heath (9D) were the last steam depots in the Manchester area. They had both closed by the end of June 1968.

One of Patricroft's Standard class 5MT 4–6–0s, no. 73157, is seen shunting vans at Manchester Exchange station on a misty 9 March 1968. This station was connected to Manchester Victoria station by the longest platform in the UK (see the photographs on pages 28 and 29). Exchange station, which was originally opened by the London & North Western Railway (LNWR) in 1884, closed in 1969.

This photograph, taken on 18 November 1967, shows one of Carnforth's (10A) 'Black Five' 4–6–0s, no. 45017, shunting a van train at the east end of Manchester Victoria station. This Lancashire & Yorkshire Railway (L&YR) station opened in 1844. It was completely modernised in the mid-1990s, when the Manchester Arena was built above the north side of the station, but the station still retained its nineteenth-century façade and concourse.

On summer Saturdays in 1965, there were still many holiday trains hauled by steam traction, none more so than the Wolverhampton (Low Level) trains to the south and south-west resorts of England. Ex-GWR 'Grange' class 4–6–0 no. 6855 (formerly *Saighton Grange*) is seen leaving Hunting Butts tunnel, just north of Cheltenham, on 31 July 1965 with the 06.55 (Saturdays only) Wolverhampton (LL) to Penzance train. These popular and powerful locomotives were designed by C.B. Collett and built between 1936 and 1939.

This also shows the 06.55 (SO) Wolverhampton to Penzance train, this time leaving Cheltenham Malvern Road station on 26 June 1965. In charge is 'Grange' class 4–6–0 no. 6827 (formerly *Llanfrecha Grange*). By this time, most of the ex-GWR locomotives had been shorn of their cabside number-plates and, if named, their name-plates. (*Both photographs: Ben Ashworth*)

Another popular destination for holiday trains to and from Wolverhampton (LL) was the Dorset resort of Weymouth. On 24 July 1965, BR Standard class 5MT no. 73020 passes Brewham signal-box on the GWR West of England main line with the 10.45 from Wolverhampton to Weymouth. At Castle Cary, the train will leave the main line and take the line to Yeovil (Pen Mill) and then on to Weymouth. The BR Standard Class 5MT 4–6–0s were designed at Doncaster and introduced in 1951. (*Hugh Ballantyne*)

The final photograph in this summer Saturday quartet shows ex-GWR 'Modified Hall' class 4–6–0 no. 6983 (formerly *Otterington Hall*) as it runs through Grimstone & Frampton station at 11.45 a.m. on 17 July 1965 with a relief Wolverhampton (LL) to Weymouth train. This location is near Maiden Newton, south of Yeovil. The 'Hall' class 4–6–0s were designed by Collett and introduced in 1928, but the 'Modified Hall' class 4–6–0s were introduced in 1944, and were a Hawksworth development of the earlier Collett design. (*Peter Gray*)

The Locomotive Club of Great Britain (LCGB) ran an 'East Devon Tour' on Sunday 28 February 1965. The tour left Waterloo at 09.02, ran to Yeovil Junction and on to Axminster, from where there were two parties, covering Lyme Regis and Seaton or Seaton and Sidmouth branches, Tipton St Johns, Exmouth and Exeter Central for the return journey to Waterloo. A variety of steam locomotive power was used, including a pair of Ivatt class 2MT 2–6–2Ts nos 41206 and 41291, seen here crossing Cannington viaduct on the return journey from Lyme Regis. This tour was repeated the following Sunday (7 March) because of the demand for tickets. (*Hugh Ballantyne*)

'Castle' class 4–6–0 no. 7029 *Clun Castle* pauses at Westbury station on 23 May 1965 with a return special train organised by the Stephenson Locomotive Society (SLS) from Exeter to Birmingham via Bath and Yate South Junction, the outward journey from Birmingham (Snow Hill) to Exeter having been run via Reading, Basingstoke and Salisbury. (*Hugh Ballantyne*)

On 27 March 1965, class 2MT 2–6–2Ts nos 41206 and 41291 approach Yarde Halt (south of Torrington) with the Exeter to Barnstaple section of the 'Exmoor Ranger' special charter train, organised jointly by the RCTS and the Plymouth Railway Circle. This special also ran from Barnstaple to Ilfracombe and return, which was the last steam working out of this popular north Devon seaside resort. It then ran back to Exeter via the former GWR route to Taunton. From Ilfracombe to Barnstaple and Exeter, the train engine was ex-GWR class 2251 0–6–0 no. 3205 (now preserved), with the 2–6–2T locomotives providing banking assistance out of Ilfracombe. No. 3205 had earlier provided banking assistance out of Braunton, and then followed from Mortehoe down to Ilfracombe. (*Peter Gray*)

To celebrate the former London & South Western Railway (LSWR) Launceston branch centenary, 1865–1965, a special train was organised by the Great Western Society (South West Group) on 5 September 1965. The special train, hauled by 2–6–2T no. 41283, is seen leaving Dunsland Cross station (between Holsworth and Halwill Junction) with the eastbound centenary special. (*Peter Gray*)

Ex-LMS 'Jubilee' class 4–6–0 no. 45593 *Kholapur* approaches Blea Moor sidings, on the Settle to Carlisle route, with the 09.20 London St Pancras to Glasgow train on Saturday 19 August 1967. No. 45593, which worked the Leeds to Carlisle section of this train, was shedded, together with the few remaining members of the class, at Leeds Holbeck (55A). (*Ken Hale*)

In May 1967, 'Black Five' 4–6–0 no. 45013 is caught by the camera as it climbs the last few yards of the 1 in 100 up to Ais Gill summit with a southbound freight from Carlisle to Leeds. Dominating the background is the notable S&C landmark of Wild Boar Fell. (*Ken Hale*)

Class 8F 2 8 0 no. 48090 gives out a magnificent plume of exhaust as it pulls through Appleby on 4 November 1967 with a southbound anhydrite train from Long Meg quarry sidings, and at the same time passes a northbound freight working. Through steam working finished on the S&C route at the end of 1967. (*Ken Hale*)

The last rays of the setting sun glint on class 5MT 4–6–0 no. 44766 as it performs shunting duties at the eastern end of Llandudno Junction station on Wednesday 7 September 1966.

Opposite top: The splendid gantry signal at the eastern end of Rhyl station frames 'Britannia' Pacific no. 70004, formerly *William Shakespeare*, as it leaves the North Wales coastal resort and heads for Crewe and Euston with the return working of the 'Conway Valley' tour on 24 September 1966 (see also photograph on page 61). Note also the LNWR signal-box on the right-hand side. (*Ken Hale*)

Opposite below: On 7 June 1965, class 5MT 2–6–0 no. 42819 hurries along near Deganwy (just south of Llandudno) with a Llandudno to Manchester empty coaching stock train. These ex-LMS 2–6–0s were introduced in 1926, and were designed by George Hughes (formerly of the Lancashire & Yorkshire Railway), and subsequently built under the direction of Sir Henry Fowler, who took over from Hughes as the LMS Chief Mechanical Engineer in 1925. (*Ken Hale*)

The Somerset & Dorset line (S&DJR) was originally scheduled to close on 3 January 1966, but this was rescinded at the last hour because of the lack of replacement bus services.

Over the weekend of 1 and 2 January 1966, two special trains had been organised by the LCGB and RCTS respectively to mark the closure with last runs over the line. The LCGB special which ran on 1 January was called the 'Mendip Merchantman', and ran from Waterloo hauled by SR 'Merchant Navy' Pacific no. 35011 *General Steam Navigation*. This locomotive came off at Templecombe, to be replaced by Ivatt 2–6–2Ts nos 41307 and 41238 for a trip down the Highbridge branch, and they are seen here approaching Evercreech Junction with the Highbridge section of the special train.

The RCTS tour the following day (2 January) was hauled by U class 2–6–0 no. 31638 and unrebuilt 'West Country' Pacific no. 34015 *Exmouth*. The special train is seen crossing over Prestleigh viaduct (halfway between Evercreech Junction and Shepton Mallet) as it heads for Bath on the outward journey from London. Prestleigh viaduct was demolished in January 1993. (*Both photographs: Hugh Ballantyne*)

The S&D finally closed on Monday 7 March 1966, and several special trains were organised for the final weekend.

On Saturday 5 March, the Great Western Society special train pulls out of Bath Green Park terminus at the start of its journey to Bournemouth and return. Hauling the train is, appropriately, 8F 2–8–0 no. 48706 off Bath Green Park shed (82F). On the same day there was also a special charter organised by the LCGB. This train was photographed crossing Tuckingmill viaduct, just south of Combe Down tunnel, on the return journey from Bath. In charge of the train are a pair of immaculate unrebuilt SR Pacifics, 'West Country' no. 34006 *Bude* and 'Battle of Britain' no. 34057 *Biggin Hill*. These locomotives were designed by Bulleid, and introduced in 1945 and 1946 respectively. (*Both photographs: Hugh Ballantyne*)

The 12.35 Waterloo to Weymouth train passes through Upwey & Broadwey station on 17 July 1965 with SR rebuilt 'West Country' Pacific no. 34009 *Lyme Regis* in charge. In the foreground is the trackbed of the former GWR branch line to Abbotsbury, which closed in 1952. Upwey & Broadwey station was originally named Upwey Junction, but changed on the closure of the branch line. Note also the branch platform still *in situ*. (*Peter Gray*)

On 15 October 1966, the down 'Bournemouth Belle', with SR rebuilt 'West Country' Pacific no. 34037 *Clovelly* in charge, speeds through the old LSWR four-track section just to the west of Winchfield station. As can be seen, electrification of the trackwork is proceeding apace, and would be in full use on the Bournemouth route by July of the following year. (*Ken Hale*)

Ex-SR 'Merchant Navy' Pacific no. 35014 *Nederland Line* (fortunately still with its name-plate) passes through Redbridge (near Southampton) on 30 December 1966 with the 11.07 Bournemouth to Waterloo train. (*Hugh Ballantyne*)

Pirbright cutting is the location as BR Standard class 5MT 4–6–0 no. 73022 heads towards Waterloo with an up midday passenger working on 10 September 1966. Once again, as with the previous two scenes, signs of electrification are evident.

The watering of locomotives at or near the ends of station platforms was once a common sight in the days of steam traction. This was often a very speedy movement with no time wasted, with the fireman (who was also, coincidentally, the younger member of the footplate crew) being in charge of this duty, while the driver observed the water gauges.

Above: On 26 February 1968, 'Black Five' 4–6–0 no. 44890 takes water at Preston station before leaving with the 12.17 train to Manchester Victoria station.

Opposite top: A4 Pacific no. 60019 *Bittern* takes water at Perth station on 16 June 1966, before leaving with the 17.15 Aberdeen to Glasgow three-hour train. With an arrival at Perth at 18.51 and departure at 18.56, the crew have little time for this operation and, as can be seen, both fireman and driver are involved. Note also the station entrance (long since closed) from St Leonards bridge to the main up platform.

Opposite below: The third photograph in this sequence shows ex-GWR class 5700 0–6–0PT no. 8718 taking water at Halesowen on 12 March 1966. The water tank was situated a few yards to the east of the station at the start of the truncated Longbridge section of the line, the line to Longbridge having closed in 1963.

'Britannia' Pacific no. 70025 *Western Star* hurries over Dillicar water troughs to the south of Tebay with a northbound passenger train on Saturday 15 July 1967. (*Ken Hale*)

Opposite: Two more scenes at Dillicar in the beautiful Lune Valley, both taken on 16 September 1966. The first, taken in the early afternoon, shows 'Black Five' 4–6–0 no. 44892 on a southbound breakdown train, which includes what looks like an ex-LNWR coach.

A little later, and 'Black Five' 4–6–0 no. 44906 approaches with an up goods train. For all three views, the photographers are standing on, or close to, what is now the M6 motorway.

During 1966, the former LMS North Wales main line between Chester and Holyhead still saw a variety of steam working, particularly passenger workings between Manchester Victoria station and Bangor/Holyhead, mainly using class 5MT 4–6–0s of both LMS and BR Standard construction.

Left: BR Standard class 5MT no. 73035 as it leaves Conway station on 7 September 1966 with a morning Manchester to Bangor train. At the time, this locomotive was shedded at Manchester Patricroft (9H).

Below: Another Patricroft BR Standard 4–6–0, no. 73094, skirts round the edge of the beautiful Conway Castle and approaches Conway tubular bridge with a Bangor to Manchester Victoria train on the early evening of 5 September 1966.

Opposite: This view, taken at 5.50 p.m., a few minutes earlier than the previous scene, shows ex-LMS 'Black Five' 4–6–0 no. 45042 with a Euston to Holyhead train, steam traction having taken over at Crewe. At the rear of the train is the castellated entrance to Conway tubular bridge. Note also the BR lineside man – no 'visi-vests' in those days!

Tablet exchange at Old Hill. This photograph was taken on the Halesowen branch near Old Hill station on 19 August 1966. Ex-GWR class 5700 0–6–0PT no. 4646 has just banked a Halesowen to Langley freight up the steep bank out of Halesowen, which is hauled by ex-LMS class 2MT 2–6–0 no. 46470.

On 6 October 1966, class 2MT 2–6–0 no. 46442, shedded at Tyseley (2A), climbs the steep gradient at Amblecote (near Stourbridge shed) with a Stourbridge to Dudley freight working. By now, Stourbridge shed had closed to steam, and Tyseley would close on 7 November 1966, thus bringing to an end steam workings on the Stourbridge to Dudley line, as well as the Old Hill to Halesowen branch. The ex-LMS class 2MT 2–6–0s were designed by Ivatt and introduced in 1946.

The BR Standard class 2MT 2–6–0s, which were similar in appearance to the Ivatt 2–6–0s, were introduced in 1953 and designed at Derby.

No. 78001 (*above*) is seen at Woodchester on the Nailsworth branch on 3 May 1965, with the Mondays/Wednesdays/Fridays only Nailsworth goods train. This former Midland Railway branch line ran south-eastwards from Stonehouse on the Bristol to Gloucester main line.

The second photograph on the Nailsworth branch (*below*) shows 2–6–0 no. 78004 at Nailsworth on 28 April 1965. No. 78004 has just reversed off the water tank siding, and the fireman is about to switch points for access to the goods yard. (*Both photographs: Ben Ashworth*)

On 30 July 1966, ex-LMS 'Jubilee' class 4–6–0 no. 45565 *Victoria*, shedded at Low Moor (56F) just south of Bradford, approaches Salwick station on the four-track section of the Blackpool to Preston line. The train is a return Blackpool to Bradford summer Saturday service. Just to the east of this station are Lea Road water troughs (see the photographs on pages 138 and 139). No. 45565 was withdrawn from service in January 1967.

Ex-SR 'West Country' Pacific no. 34046 *Braunton* takes water at Southampton Central station on 30 August 1965, before leaving with the 13.30 Waterloo to Weymouth train. Dominating this classic scene is the splendid SR signal gantry. Note also the typical SR station lamps of concrete construction. (*Hugh Ballantyne*)

Another fine signal gantry, this time the GWR gantry at the northern end of Shrewsbury station. On 25 October 1966, class 8F 2–8–0 no. 48738 heads north-west to Crewe with a mixed-goods train. The line to Crewe swings away to the right, while the line to Chester is straight ahead.

These two photographs were taken on the early evening of 26 July 1966 at Hatton bank on the former GWR Leamington Spa to Birmingham (Snow Hill) main line.

The first shows class 8F 2–8–0 no. 48122 on the down slow line with a neat-looking mixed-goods train bound for the Birmingham area. A few minutes later, another 8F 2–8–0, this time no. 48351, passes with an empty car-carrier train, possibly from Southampton Docks to the Austin Motor Co. at Longbridge.

On 24 July 1965, 'Britannia' Pacific no. 70045 *Lord Rowallan* tackles the 1 in 108 at the eastern end of Hatton bank with the 11.05 (Saturdays only) Weymouth to Wolverhampton (Low Level) train. (*Ken Hale*)

Veteran former North British Railway class J36 0–6–0 no. 65345 has just left Edinburgh Waverley station and is running through Princes Street Gardens on 27 August 1966 with a special train organised by the Railway Society of Scotland, Edinburgh area. This tour, the proceeds of which went to the J36 Preservation Fund, covered many of the branch lines in and around Edinburgh, including Corstorphine, Leith East and North, Musselburgh and Smeaton. The class J36 0–6–0 locomotives were designed by Holmes, and introduced in 1888. One member of the class was preserved, no. 673 (65243) *Maude*, by the Scottish Railway Preservation Society, Falkirk. (*Ken Hale*)

Two more pre-grouping locomotives are seen on the evening of 29 July 1966 at Dundee Tay Bridge shed (62B): ex-NB class J37 0–6–0s nos 64547 and 64620. This class was introduced in 1914, and designed by Reid. Unlike the class J36, no members of this class have been preserved. (*Ken Hale*)

The vintage locomotives seen on the facing page (*lower*) are pictured at work in these two photographs.

On 15 June 1966, no. 64620 (*above*) crosses the Montrose basin as it leaves Montrose with the return afternoon goods to Dundee. The train is just leaving the first (and northerly) of the two viaducts which cross this river basin. This viaduct is of metal construction, the southerly one being built of brick.

The second view (*below*), also taken on 15 June 1966, shows no. 64547 engaged in shunting duties at Brechin station. In a short while, it will be leaving with the daily goods train to Montrose.

Clustered round the Ransomes & Rapier turntable in Saltley shed (21A) on Sunday 15 May 1966 are BR Standard class 9F 2–10–0s nos 92164 and 92104, and 'Black Five' 4–6–0 no. 45349. This large locomotive depot (formerly Midland Railway) consisted of several sheds, and this picture shows no. 3 shed. The shed had an allocation of steam locomotives until the end of steam in the Birmingham area in December 1966.

Once the pride of Stewarts Lane shed (75D), and on this occasion still clean but unadorned, 'Britannia' Pacific no. 70004 (formerly *William Shakespeare*) stands outside Salisbury shed (72B) on 14 August 1966, before working part of the LCGB 'A2 Commemorative Tour'. This tour ran from Waterloo to Exeter Central via Salisbury and Yeovil Junction, and returned to Waterloo via the former GWR main line to Westbury and then to Salisbury and Waterloo. Former LNER class A2 Pacific no. 60532 *Blue Peter* was in charge of the tour from Waterloo to Exeter and on to Westbury, where no. 70004 took over for the return to Waterloo. (*Hugh Ballantyne*)

GWR and LMS shunting locomotives at Chester shed (6A) on 20 August 1966. Ex-GWR class 5700 0–6–0PT no. 9630 basks in the sunshine as former LMS class 3F 0–6–0T no. 47598 slumbers inside the shed. The class 3Fs were introduced on the LMS in 1924, and were a development of a Midland Railway design. They were popularly known as 'Jinties'. Several members of the class have been preserved. (*Hugh Ballantyne*)

These three scenes were taken on the Great Central Railway (GCR) in the summer of 1966, just before the end of the through workings between Marylebone and Nottingham on 3 September 1966.

The first photograph, taken on 13 August 1966, shows 'Black Five' 4–6–0 no. 45289 emerging from Catesby tunnel (Northamptonshire) with the 10.57 Nottingham to Neasden sidings van train. (*Ken Blocksidge/Roger Siviter collection*)

Opposite top: The 10.57 Nottingham to Neasden van train, this time taken at Brackley viaduct on 3 September 1966, with class 5MT 4–6–0 no. 45292 in charge. This impressive viaduct had twenty-two arches, and was 320ft long. It was finally demolished in 1978.

Opposite below: Ex-LMS class 8F 2–8–0 no. 48192 leaving Nottingham Victoria station and approaching Mansfield Road tunnel on 1 September 1966 with a northbound load of coal. Behind the train is the GCR Victoria North signal-box.

These four photographs were taken at Carlisle station on the afternoon of Wednesday 30 March 1966, and give some idea of the steam activity still to be found in this large station, once home to many pre-grouping railway companies.

In the first picture (*above*) Ivatt class 2MT 2–6–2T no. 41264 shunts empty stock out of platform 1. Note the station trolleys. On the eastern side of the station, another Ivatt 2–6–2T, no. 41217, is engaged in shunting duties (*below*).

A few minutes after the previous photograph, and light engine 'Britannia' Pacific no. 70046 *Anzac* runs through the station on its way to its home shed at Carlisle Kingmoor (12A). This shed is on the east side of the WCML, about 1½ miles north of Carlisle station.

The final scene on this blustery March afternoon shows 'Black Five' 4–6–0 no. 44854 (off Leeds Holbeck shed, 55A) waiting to leave one of the station's bay platforms with the 16.37 train to Bradford, via the Settle & Carlisle route.

On 12 March 1966, class 8F 2–8–0 no. 48665 approaches Brymbo with a freight working from Croes Newydd yard, Wrexham. (*Ken Hale*)

A neat-looking southbound mixed-freight train hauled by ex-LMS class 8F 2–8–0 no. 48754 approaches Cosford, on the former GWR Wolverhampton to Shrewsbury line, at 12.20 p.m. on Wednesday 26 January 1967. The line here runs past RAF Cosford, which is also home to the famous aero museum. Within a few weeks, with the end of the through workings between Paddington and Birkenhead on 5 March 1967, steam would finish on this route.

Our final class 8F photograph shows no. 48225 near Waverton on the Chester to Crewe line with an up goods train on 17 October 1966. Note the mix of permanent way huts, the earlier design on the left and the one of BR construction on the right. At the time, no. 48225 was shedded at Kirkby-in-Ashfield (16E), Nottinghamshire, so this freight may have been bound for the East Midlands via Kidsgrove and Stoke-on-Trent.

On a misty autumn day (4 October 1966) 'Black Five' 4–6–0 no. 45264 gives out a hearty exhaust as it leaves Wrexham and heads for Shrewsbury with a heavy van train.

Ivatt class 2MT 2–6–2T no. 41241 runs through the eastern side of the Skipton station area after shunting coal wagons in the adjacent yard. Note the fine Victorian railway buildings, and also the MR signal-box on the left-hand side. In the background is the 'Sylko' mill, complete with its tall chimney. The date is 11 July 1966.

This photograph was taken at the western end of Skipton station on 23 June 1966. Ex-LMS class 3F 'Jinty' 0–6–0T no. 47427 pauses during shunting duties, while ex-WD class 8F 2–8–0 no. 90345 runs by with an up coal train. Off to the left-hand side was situated Skipton shed (10G), which closed in 1967. In its heyday it had an allocation of thirty-six engines, with ex-LMS class 4F 0–6–0s being the predominant locomotives. (*Ben Ashworth*)

With the end of through workings between Paddington and Birkenhead during the weekend of 4/5 March 1967, several special steam charter trains were run to mark the event. These two photographs, taken on 5 March 1966 near Codsall station on the Wolverhampton to Shrewsbury line, show class 5MT 4–6–0 no. 44680 with the outward journey of the second of two Stephenson Locomotive Society (Midland Area) specials from Birmingham to Birkenhead and return. The first special train was worked by ex-GWR 'Castle' class 4–6–0 no. 7029 *Clun Castle*. Note the characteristic 'pose' of the fireman.

Another last-day working and also, in this case, the closure of the line. On 30 April 1967, class J94 0–6–0STs nos 68012 and 68006 head an SLS special on the last day of the Cromford & High Peak Railway (C&HPR). The location is near Middleton Top at the start of the 1 in 14 of Hopton incline. These ex-WD locomotives were introduced in 1943 and designed by Riddles, and were purchased by the LNER in 1946.

This photograph was taken on the day that England won the World Cup – 30 July 1966. Ex-LMS class 5MT 4–6–0 no. 45080, with a return Blackpool to Leeds and Bradford summer Saturday train, speeds over Lea Road water troughs near Salwick on the Blackpool to Preston line on the afternoon of that famous day.

A few minutes later, another 'Black Five', no. 45350, passes with an up passenger train.

By the spring of 1968, the four-track section of the Blackpool to Preston line had been reduced to double track. This is very evident in this view of 'Black Five' 4–6–0 no. 45025 as it hurries along near Salwick with a Blackpool to Manchester parcels train on 10 April 1968. As was to be expected of this once-numerous class, many LMS 'Black Five' 4–6–0 locomotives have been preserved, including no. 45025, which was privately preserved at the Strathspey Railway, Boat of Garten. Also, over the years no. 45025 has worked many steam charter trains throughout the BR Scottish Region. (*Hugh Ballantyne*)

A very grimy ex-LMS class 8F 2–8–0 no. 48124 is seen near Silverdale on the Furness line, heading for Carnforth with an up tank train at midday on 17 April 1968. The Furness line from Carnforth to Barrow saw steam action right until the very end.

Another area that still had steam workings almost to the end, and certainly until the beginning of June 1968, was that around Stockport, notably the Cheshire Lines Committee (CLC) route between Widnes and Stockport. On 25 April 1968, class 8F 2–8–0 no. 48765 has just passed Skelton Junction (at the rear of the train) and is heading towards Stockport with a lengthy train of coal empties from the Widnes direction. Note the shed code 9F – Heaton Mersey (near Stockport).

We complete this trio of 8F portraits with a photograph taken at Hagley (on the Stourbridge Junction to Kidderminster line) on the evening of 12 May 1966. The ex-LMS 2–8–0 no. 48424 has just pulled through the station and is heading north with the 20.10 Kidderminster to Oxley (Wolverhampton) goods train. I took this photograph from Hagley signal-box by kind permission of the friendly signalman.

The next two photographs were taken at Rose Grove shed (10F), Burnley on 19 July 1968, a few days before closure. The first scene (*above*) shows class 8F 2–8–0s nos 48723 and 48167 by the coaling tower, and the second (*opposite top*) shows 8F no. 48393 and several 'Black Five' 4–6–0s outside the shed.

Our final photograph was taken at the very end of BR steam, on the evening of Sunday 11 August 1968 at Carnforth shed yard, and shows a line-up of locomotives awaiting preservation, including BR Standard class 4MT 4–6–0 no. 75027, ex-LMS Fairburn class 4MT 2–6–4T no. 42085, ex-LNER class B1 4–6–0 no. 61306, Ivatt class 2MT 2–6–0 no. 46441 and Fairburn 2–6–4T no. 42073.

Bibliography

Gammell, Chris, *Steam Sheds & Their Locomotives*, Ian Allan, 1995
Siviter, Roger, *Waverley: Portrait of a Famous Route*, Runpast, 1988
——, *Farewell to Steam*, Sutton Publishing, 2003
Stephenson, Brian, *Great Western 4–6–0s*, Ian Allan, 1984
——, *BR Standard Steam Locomotives*, Ian Allan, 1984
Last Years of British Steam, vols 1 and 2, first series compiled by G. Freeman Allen, Ian Allan, 1967 and 1972
Railway Magazine
Railway World
Various *Past & Present* volumes, Silver Link

Index